# Awakened in the Mirror

a Devotional

Remonica Washington

©Copyright 2025 Remonica Washington

All rights reserved. This book is protected under the copyright laws of the United States of America.

ISBN: 978-1-954609-91-4

No portion of this book may be reproduced, distributed, or transmitted in any form, including photocopying, recording, or other electronic or mechanical methods, without the written permission of the publisher, except in the case of brief quotations embodied in reviews and certain other non-commercial uses permitted by copyright law. Permission granted on request.

For information regarding special discounts for bulk purchases, please contact LaBoo Publishing Enterprise at staff@laboopublishing.com.

Scripture taken from the New King James Version®. Copyright © 1982 by Thomas Nelson. Used by permission. All rights reserved.

The Holy Bible, King James Version. Cambridge Edition: 1769; King James Bible Online, 2019. www.kingjamesbibleonline.org.

Scripture quotations marked (NLT) are taken from the Holy Bible, New Living Translation, copyright ©1996, 2004, 2015 by Tyndale House Foundation. Used by permission of Tyndale House Publishers, Inc., Carol Stream, Illinois 60188. All rights reserved.

New Revised Standard Version Bible, copyright © 1989 National Council of the Churches of Christ in the United States of America. Used by permission. All rights reserved worldwide.

Scripture quotations marked (NIV) are taken from the Holy Bible, New International Version®, NIV®. Copyright © 1973, 1978, 1984, 2011 by Biblica, Inc.™ Used by permission of Zondervan. All rights reserved worldwide. www.zondervan.com

Scripture quotations marked ESV are from the Holy Bible, English Standard Version, copyright © 2001 by Crossway Bibles, a publishing ministry of Good News Publishers. Used by permission. All rights reserved.

# Awakened in the Mirror

## What Do You See When You Look in the Mirror?

Beyond the reflection lies a deeper truth – one of grace, purpose, and divine design. Through intimate personal stories, *Awakened in the Mirror* invites you on a journey of self-discovery, where each reflection reveals God's goodness and the beauty of your unique creation.

# Dedication

To my forbearing husband — thank you for standing beside me, encouraging my dreams, and covering me with unwavering support and love.

To my son and precious grands — you are my joy, my heartbeat, and the living reminders of God's goodness. May you always chase God's purpose, live boldly, and trust God's perfect plan for your lives.

This book is for you — my heart, my legacy, my inspiration.

# Acknowledgments

To my amazing mother, Shi'Rae — thank you for lovingly displaying strength through every struggle and sacrifice. Your courage became my blueprint; your love, my safe place.

To my beloved maternal grandparents in Heaven — I carry your wise lessons and love with me daily. Thank you for never giving up on Mom and me, for planting seeds of faith and resilience that still bloom in my life today.

No mistakes, no failures — only God's perfect timing and unfailing grace. Every step of this journey is proof that with Him, even our hardest seasons become holy ground.

# From the Author

Every page of Awakened in the Mirror was written with you in mind — the woman, the man, the soul who knows there's more but isn't sure how to reach it. I know the weight of fear, the sting of doubt, and the ache of unanswered prayers. I've stood where the mirror reflected everything except who I truly was in Christ. My hope is that through these words you will find courage to face your own reflection with truth, grace, and renewed faith. May this journey remind you: you are not stuck, you are being stirred. And if you move with God, everything in you — and around you — can be transformed.

# Table of Contents

Introduction . . . . . . . . . . . . . . . . . . . . . . . . .xiii

Who's Holding Your Arms? . . . . . . . . . . . . . . . . . . 1

W.A.I.T: Who Am I Trusting? . . . . . . . . . . . . . . . . .7

You Win When You Can Accept Losing . . . . . . . . . 11

Release Your Made-It Mindset . . . . . . . . . . . . . . . 15

When Jesus' Name Is All You Need . . . . . . . . . . . . 21

The Escape Is Near . . . . . . . . . . . . . . . . . . . . . . . 25

Follow God's Path for You . . . . . . . . . . . . . . . . . . 29

Don't Fear Embarrassment . . . . . . . . . . . . . . . . . 33

You Don't Know My Prayers . . . . . . . . . . . . . . . . 37

It Will Pass . . . . . . . . . . . . . . . . . . . . . . . . . . . . . 41

That's Not My Story . . . . . . . . . . . . . . . . . . . . . . 47

I'm Courageous, Not Crazy . . . . . . . . . . . . . . . . . 53

Circle It . . . . . . . . . . . . . . . . . . . . . . . . . . . . . . . 57

Choosing Kindness. . . . . . . . . . . . . . . . . . . . . . . 61

You Can Soar!. . . . . . . . . . . . . . . . . . . . . . . . . . 65

Stop Apologizing For Your Uniqueness . . . . . . . . . 69

Activate Your Trust, Then Wait Patiently. . . . . . . . . 73

Father or Daddy?. . . . . . . . . . . . . . . . . . . . . . . . 77

Serving an Uncommon God . . . . . . . . . . . . . . . . 81

Seasons of the Unexpected: Finding Purpose in Pain. . . 85

Don't Starve Your Spirit — Feed Your Soul Daily . . . . . 89

Life's Chaos, God's Control . . . . . . . . . . . . . . . . . 93

All Is Not Lost . . . . . . . . . . . . . . . . . . . . . . . . . 97

Remove: Letting Go of What Hinders . . . . . . . . . . 101

Reboot: A Fresh Start in the Spirit . . . . . . . . . . . . 105

Remember Who Holds Your Future . . . . . . . . . . . 109

It Could Be Worse . . . . . . . . . . . . . . . . . . . . . . 113

Don't Waste Your Grace!. . . . . . . . . . . . . . . . . . 117

It's Simple — WAS . . . . . . . . . . . . . . . . . . . . . 121

Changing Bad Behaviors. . . . . . . . . . . . . . . . . . 125

Embrace — You Changed . . . . . . . . . . . . . . . . . 129

It Was All a Dream . . . . . . . . . . . . . . . . . . . . . 135

Scared Little Girl from Louisiana. . . . . . . . . . . . . 141

# Introduction

Welcome to the profound journey of understanding your mirror, a sacred reflection of your innermost self and divine guidance. As envisioned by Remonica, a seasoned life coach, motivator, mentor, and biblical counselor, the mirror serves as more than just a physical object—it's a gateway to spiritual enlightenment and communion with the divine. In the realm of self-discovery, the mirror becomes a conduit for hearing the whispers of God and unraveling the mysteries of existence. Through introspection and contemplation, we embark on a transformative odyssey, delving deep into the recesses of our souls to uncover hidden truths and divine revelations.

Scripture enlightens us in Psalm 139:23-24 (NIV): "Search me, O God, and know my heart; test me and know my anxious thoughts. See if there is any offensive way in me and lead me in the way everlasting." This verse encapsulates the essence of personal reflection and self-evaluation, inviting us to surrender to divine scrutiny and embrace the journey toward spiritual wholeness.

As Remonica guides us on this sacred voyage, let us open our hearts to the wisdom that awaits within the depths of our reflections. May we heed the gentle whispers of the divine, navigate the corridors of our souls with courage and grace, and emerge enlightened, empowered, and renewed. Together, let us embark on the path of understanding our mirror, where the divine meets the human, and the soul finds its true reflection.

# Who's Holding Your Arms?

In 2008, I was diagnosed with myasthenia gravis (MG), an autoimmune condition that weakens muscles throughout the body. If you think about it, our entire body relies on muscles—every movement, every breath, even the ability to speak or swallow. For me, MG has significantly limited the mobility of my arms. Simple daily tasks—getting dressed, cleaning, worshipping, doing my hair, reaching for something, holding a bottle, shaving—have become challenges.

Yet, just like Moses, God has provided me with an unwavering, patient, and willing vessel—my husband, who helps me with these essential needs without complaint. Thank You, Lord, for knowing exactly what I need and sending someone to lift my arms when I cannot.

Today, I want to encourage you to be an arm-lifter—or to walk closely with those who can lift your arms when you are weary. Someone like Aaron and Hur, faithful companions who will go to the mountaintop with you just to help hold your arms up. An arm-lifter isn't just someone who supports you in easy moments. They challenge you in your wrongs, equip you with wisdom and knowledge, and walk alongside you when the road is uncertain. Sometimes, they sit in silence with you—simply being present.

Make it your mission to live as an arm-holder like Aaron or Hur. Serve as a spiritual mentor, a steady presence, and a beacon of faith. Seek out opportunities to lift others up—pray for someone in need, offer a meal to a struggling family, speak life with a kind word or a warm hug, give a ride, pay a bill, or listen without judgment.

Behind the fake smiles and tinted windows, people are crying out for help—silently suffering, exhausted from unseen battles, drained from neglect, and weary from holding everything together alone. Let's not be too busy to notice. Masking is overrated. Genuine love is what the world is longing for.

Orchestrate divine connections—trusted relationships that remind us we don't have to bear our burdens alone. Ask God to strengthen us to hold others up when they grow weary, so that no one's arms fall from lack of support.

Even today, Moses' story shows us interdependence, humility, and divine strategy. Moses was a powerful prophet, yet he needed help. Even the strongest spiritual leaders get weary, and the most faithful prayer warriors grow tired. But God sends people—Aaron and Hur types—to help sustain the weight.

You may be a Moses today, your arms trembling from the load. Or maybe you're called to be an Aaron or a Hur—to notice, to act, to lift. Remember, both roles are sacred, and God designed battles to be won through collaboration, not isolation.

God's presence was on that mountaintop—not just in the miracle of victory, but in the quiet strength of brotherhood. May we each walk in the wisdom to lead, the humility to receive help, and the courage to lift another's arms until the battle is won.

### Scriptural Reflection:

Exodus 17:12 (NIV): "When Moses' hands grew tired... Aaron and Hur held his hands up—one on one side, one on the other—so that his hands remained steady till sunset."

### Spiritual Reflection:

Imagine standing on a mountaintop, your arms stretched toward heaven as a physical act of intercession for your people. You are Moses—chosen by God, leading a nation, bearing the weight of responsibility. Below, Joshua fights the Amalekites. Around you, the wind blows, the sun beats down, and your arms begin to tremble from fatigue.

You want to keep them raised—you know that victory hinges on it—but your human strength is fading. Then, without asking, Aaron and Hur step in. They bring a stone for you to sit on, and then—one on each side—they hold up your arms. And because of their support, Israel prevails.

## Self-Reflection Question:

Are you willing to admit when you're tired and let someone hold up your arms? Are you positioned close enough to someone to notice when they're weary—and are you ready to step in? How might God be calling you to lift up a friend, leader, or loved one today?

## Reflection Prayer:

Father God, thank You for the arm-lifters in my life, who see my desire to worship with raised hands and proudly lifts them for me. Lord, in doing so, they unknowingly worships alongside me. But God, You are the One who equips Your children to be faithful leaders and supporters, just like Aaron and Hur.

**Pause. Breathe.
Write what is on your heart.**

# W.A.I.T: Who Am I Trusting?

In life, we often find ourselves placing trust in many things and people. We trust our car to start, the chair to hold us, our family and friends to show up, our relationships to last, and our doctor's diagnosis to be right. Trust becomes the thread that binds our expectations, yet how often are we let down? Friends might disappoint, marriages falter, cars break down, and doctors misdiagnose, so our expectations fall short. The question is, who are we truly trusting? Are we placing our trust in things and people prone to error—or in the One who is eternally faithful?

## Understanding Trust:

*Spiritual Trust:* In a spiritual sense, trust means surrendering completely to God, believing that He will guide, protect, and provide. It's rooted in the faith that God knows all things and has our best interests in mind, even when we can't see the full picture.

*Secular Trust:* In a more worldly sense, trust is often based on proven reliability. We trust people and things based on patterns of consistency, competence, and experience. However, this form of trust is conditional and limited by human fallibility.

## Scriptural Reflection:

Proverbs 3:5–6 (NIV): "Trust in the Lord with all your heart and lean not on your own understanding; in all your ways submit to him, and he will make your paths straight."

## Spiritual Reflection:

Abraham: When God asked Abraham to leave his homeland and go to a place he didn't know, Abraham trusted God's direction without question (Genesis 12:1–4). His faith was tested further when God asked him to sacrifice his son Isaac, but Abraham continued to trust that God's promises would stand (Genesis 22).

## Self-Reflection Question:

When faced with uncertainty or doubt, do I pause to ask myself if I am trusting in God's promises—or am I leaning on my own understanding?

### Reflection Prayer:

Lord, help me to place my full trust in You, not in the fleeting stability of this world. Teach me to lean on You with my whole heart, for You are my Rock and my Refuge. Guide me by Your Spirit as I walk by faith. Amen.

Pause. Breathe.
Write what's on your heart.

# You Win When You Can Accept Losing

In life, not every win is truly good, and not every loss is truly bad. It takes spiritual maturity to realize that some of our greatest growth comes from moments that at first look like defeat. When we begin to embrace this truth, we can see losses not as setbacks but as sacred tools—tools that build our faith, shape our character, and teach us how to rise again.

Losses don't have to define you—they can develop you. Yes, disappointment hurts, and it's human to grieve, question, and feel frustrated when things don't go as planned. But those moments are also divine invitations—invitations to reflect, to pray, to grow, and to ask God, "What are You teaching me in this? How can I move forward wiser and stronger?" Because when you can accept a loss—not as a personal failure but as a stepping stone—you gain wisdom, resilience, and perspective. That, in itself, is a win. That is success.

I recently made the decision to step into early retirement. For many, that might look like a loss—walking away from a secure position, a steady income, and a familiar routine. But I've learned that walking by faith doesn't always make sense to others. It's not always flashy, but it's always fruitful when God is involved. What may look like a loss to the world is actually a bold, courageous win in the spirit. Why? Because I'm trusting God with my "next." And the truth is—He never allows you to fail when you're walking in His will. Every one of His promises is structured for a win. I'm not just leaving something behind—I'm stepping into purpose, peace, and promise.

So if you're facing a loss right now—whether it's a dream deferred, a relationship ended, or a chapter closing—don't give up. God hasn't. Life isn't meant to break you; it's meant to build you. Even in loss, you are being positioned, refined, and prepared for more.

## Scriptural Reflection:
Habakkuk 2:2–3: "Write the vision and make it plain . . . though it tarries, wait for it; because it will surely come."

## Spiritual Reflection:
Consider Peter. He was passionate, bold, and one of Jesus' closest followers. Yet in Jesus' darkest hour, Peter denied even knowing Him—not once, but three times (Luke 22:54–62). Imagine the shame and sorrow that followed. But Jesus didn't cancel Peter. He didn't cast him aside.

Instead, He restored him tenderly and intentionally—asking Peter three times, "Do you love Me?" (John 21:15–19). And then He gave Peter a charge—"Feed My sheep."

Peter's failure became fuel for his future. What once looked like a devastating loss was transformed into one of the most powerful comebacks in Scripture. Peter went on to preach with boldness, lead with strength, and help build the early church. His loss didn't disqualify him—it equipped him.

### Self-Reflection Question:
What loss in your life might God be using as a doorway to your next season of purpose—and what would it look like to fully trust Him with it?

### Reflection Prayer:
Lord, help me see losses as part of Your plan to grow and prepare me for greater things. Grant me strength to learn, to move forward, and to trust that every setback is part of a divine setup for a winning outcome. Amen.

# Pause. Breathe.
# Write what is on your heart.

# Release Your Made-It Mindset

When we think of the phrase "made it," we often imagine reaching a point in life where we feel successful, secure, and accomplished. In our society, the phrase usually means attaining significant material possessions or status—landing a prestigious job, owning a beautiful home, driving a luxury car, accumulating a large savings account, or even becoming a millionaire. For many, these visible markers define what success looks like. But is that what "made it" truly means?

Our world tends to focus on tangible achievements as a measure of success. A high-ranking job, a thriving business, impressive degrees, and luxurious lifestyles are often seen as signs that someone has "arrived." Yet, as we consider these things, we must remember that while they can bring satisfaction, it's only temporary. These treasures we accumulate on Earth—whether money, status, or possessions—don't travel with us beyond this life.

In Philippians 3:12–14, Paul, who had every reason to boast of his spiritual credentials, makes a profound statement. Despite his dedication, his spiritual "resume," and his unwavering faith, Paul humbly admits that he hasn't yet "made it." He says, "Not that I have already obtained all this, or have already arrived at my goal, but I press on to take hold of that for which Christ Jesus took hold of me." Paul understood that the true goal wasn't earthly acclaim or accomplishments. Instead, it was to draw closer to Christ, continually pressing forward and not becoming complacent.

This humility and perspective remind us that, even with a legacy of faith and works, Paul saw himself as a work in progress. He knew that as long as he was on this journey with Christ, he hadn't yet reached the ultimate goal.

Spiritually, "making it" is about our relationship with God through Christ. It's measured not by what we've achieved but by who we are in Him. The true finish line lies beyond this world—it's a heavenly destination. God calls us not to store up treasures on Earth, but to invest in our eternal lives. The ultimate goal is to reach Heaven and hear our Creator say, "Well done, my good and faithful servant" (Matthew 25:21). That is the real moment of "making it"—the eternal prize of being with God.

We must strive not to let earthly goals and material things become idols. Our purpose is not to settle for the status quo of this world, but to continually strive for a deeper relationship with God. Jesus reminds us in Matthew 6:19–21(NIV), "Do not store up for yourselves treasures on earth, where moths and vermin destroy, and where thieves break in and steal. But store up for yourselves treasures in heaven, where moths and vermin do not destroy, and where thieves do not break in and steal. For where your treasure is, there your heart will be also."

## Scriptural Reflection:

Luke 22:31-34 (NIV): "Simon, Simon, Satan has asked to sift you as wheat. But I have prayed for you, Simon, that your faith may not fail. And when you have turned back, strengthen your brothers." But he replied, "Lord, I am ready to go with you to prison and to death." Jesus answered, "I tell you, Peter, before the rooster crows today, you will deny three times that you know me."

## Spiritual Reflection:

Peter believed he had made it spiritually. As one of Jesus' closest disciples, he walked on water, witnessed miracles, and boldly declared unwavering loyalty to Christ. His confidence was rooted in proximity, passion, and performance. In Peter's mind, his dedication qualified him.

Yet Jesus lovingly exposed Peter's blind spot: self-reliance. Peter's denial of Jesus wasn't just a failure—it was a dismantling of the "I've got this" mindset. When the rooster crowed, Peter confronted a painful truth—being close to Jesus is not the same as being transformed by Him.

Sometimes the greatest shift in mindset happens when we realize that passion without dependence is not enough.

## Self-Reflection Question:

What areas of my life have I been measuring as "successful" by the world's standards, and how can I shift my focus to align more with God's eternal purpose for me?

## Reflection Prayer:

Heavenly Father, I come before You today, asking that You guide my heart and mind toward Your true purpose for me. Help me to release any mindset that places earthly accomplishments above my spiritual journey with You. Lord, help me release the "made-it" mindset and focus on my eternal purpose. Shift my heart from worldly measures to a life centered on You. Amen.

# Pause. Breathe.
# Write what is on your heart.

# When Jesus' Name Is All You Need

We often believe we need someone else's name, title, or endorsement to move forward. Whether it's a cosigner for a loan, a reference for a job, or a connection to open a door, we look for human validation to access blessings. While relationships can be helpful, don't overlook the one name that guarantees access beyond all limitations—the name of Jesus.

Yes, the name you were given at birth matters—it reflects heritage, legacy, and identity. But when you call on the name of Jesus, you activate a power that exceeds any human recommendation or reputation. His name is not only revered—it's loaded with divine authority, unmatched influence, and supernatural breakthrough.

In Isaiah 9:6, the truth was prophesied long before Jesus walked the earth. His name is the key. It opens doors you didn't knock on. It ushers in peace where chaos once ruled. It delivers healing in hopeless situations and calls things that were dead back to life. There is no room, meeting, opportunity, or spiritual atmosphere where the name of Jesus loses its power.

Sometimes our faith is unintentionally capped at the limits of our income or network. But what your paycheck can't cover, Jesus' name can command. What your connection can't open, Jesus' name can unlock.

When fear tries to grip you, remember He is Elohim Shomri—your protector. When the provision doesn't add up, He is Jehovah Jireh—your provider. And when you feel overwhelmed and under-supported, He is Jehovah Nissi—your banner and victory.

God didn't send Jesus merely to secure your eternity. His name is your authority now. And don't treat the cross like a one-time act of mercy—his resurrection power flows through His name daily. There is no "Harry," "Sally," "Moe," or "Buckwheat," as you wisely said—no human name, regardless of its influence—that can accomplish what Jesus' name does in the spiritual and natural realms.

Jesus' name doesn't just break chains—it opens floodgates. What if your next breakthrough is one bold declaration of His name away?

## Scriptural Reflection:

Acts 4:12 (NIV): "Salvation is found in no one else, for there is no other name under heaven given to mankind by which we must be saved."

## Spiritual Reflection:

Consider blind Bartimaeus (Mark 10:46–52). He was silenced by the crowd, dismissed as unworthy, and told to be quiet. But he shouted louder: "Jesus, Son of David, have mercy on me!" That cry stopped Jesus in His tracks. He didn't need status. He didn't need sight. All he needed was faith in the name. Jesus responded not just to his cry—but to the authority and persistence with which he used it. His sight was restored, and his life changed forever.

## Self-Reflection Question:

If you stopped waiting for human approval and fully embraced the spiritual authority in Jesus' name, what vision, opportunity, or healing would you pursue today?

## Reflection Prayer:

Heavenly Father, we come to You in the powerful name of Jesus, thanking You for giving us access to all we need through Him. Help us to remember that we don't need anyone else's approval or endorsement when we have Jesus' name. Lord, teach me to confidently use my God-given name, anchored in the power of Jesus' name, to seek the blessings and opportunities You have prepared for me. Guide me in faith and courage today. Amen.

**Pause. Breathe.
Write what is on your heart.**

# The Escape Is Near

There comes a moment in every journey when we must acknowledge that we've fallen—whether it's falling into temptation, falling away from purpose, or falling into the trap of pretending everything is okay. Even so, God still sees us, loves us, and calls us by name. The beauty of surrendering after a fall is found not in shame, but in the courage to rise again—free from embarrassment, unchained from guilt, and covered by grace.

You are not too far gone, and it's not too late. Escape is near. Whether you're struggling in a toxic relationship, bound by addiction (including shoes and food), wrestling with depression, consumed by materialism, or battling self-sabotaging behaviors, God's way out is always laced with hope, healing, and restoration. But first, we must be willing to take His hand.

So today, acknowledge where you are. Own your part. Seek forgiveness, surrender with your whole heart, and stand in holy expectation, knowing that escape is not just possible—it's promised.

## Scriptural Reflection:
*1 Corinthians 10:13 (NIV):* "No temptation has overtaken you except what is common to mankind. And God is faithful; he will not let you be tempted beyond what you can bear. But when you are tempted, he will also provide a way out so that you can endure it."

## Spiritual Reflection:
Think of Joseph—betrayed by his brothers, wrongfully accused, thrown into prison, and forgotten by man, but never forgotten by God. His escape didn't come overnight, but when it did, it led to purpose, promotion, and peace. Joseph didn't allow bitterness or bondage to define him—he surrendered his circumstances to God and walked in divine expectation.

## Self-Reflection Question:
What might God be trying to free me from that I've grown comfortable with?

### Reflection Prayer for Escape:

Lord, I release my grip on what's holding me back. I surrender in faith, trusting that Your escape leads to healing, freedom, and purpose. Thank You for staying with me through it all. I am ready. Amen!

**Pause. Breathe.
Write what is on your heart.**

# Follow God's Path for You

Reflecting on 2003, I recall how far my steps had strayed from God's path and will. That year, I was laid off in August, and in my "already have it figured out" mindset, I decided I'd secure another job by March 2004. In my mind, I needed an extended break. But God had other plans—better plans.

Unbeknownst to me, a dear friend had been applying for jobs on my behalf. That act of love and concern led to an unexpected call one Tuesday afternoon while I was doing what had become my norm—sleeping. The caller introduced himself, explained why he was calling, and within twenty minutes, I was hired! I started my new job in November 2003, months earlier than my plan.

So what happened to my plans? The truth is, my plans were never really my plans. God's plans were always in motion, and they were far better than I could imagine. God's way will never harm you. His plans won't fail you. Today, I'm standing in the future He prepared for me—unharmed and covered by His grace. Won't He do it?

## Scriptural Reflection:

As His Word promises in Jeremiah 29:11 (NIV), "For I know the plans I have for you," declares the Lord, "plans to prosper you and not to harm you, plans to give you hope and a future."

## Spiritual Reflection:

Think of Paul, who followed the calling God placed on him despite challenges and comparisons. Paul wasn't concerned with doing what others did; he stayed faithful to the ministry Jesus assigned—becoming a powerful instrument of God's purpose (Acts 20:24). Like Paul, we should embrace our path without looking to walk in someone else's shoes. Do others notice you're different? That's a blessing, not a burden—God created you like no one else.

## Self-Reflection Question:

Am I trusting God's unique path for my life, or am I looking to follow in the steps of others?

**Reflection Prayer:**

Lord, thank You for ordering my steps even when I don't fully understand Your plans. Help me surrender my own ideas and trust in the path You've created for me. Let me delight in the unique future You have prepared, knowing that Your way is always good. In Jesus' name, amen.

**Pause. Breathe.
Write what is on your heart.**

# Don't Fear Embarrassment

In 1986, I faced one of the most painful moments of my life. My high school friends had moved forward in their lives, but I was eighteen years old—an unwed, pregnant teenager, fresh out of high school with no job and an incredibly uncertain future. My immediate family was wrestling with feelings of shame and blame, and even in church, I felt the weight of whispers and judgment. I cried countless tears and felt overwhelmed by embarrassment.

Then, a wise grandmother spoke words that changed everything. She looked at me with understanding and said, "You might see this as a mistake, but God doesn't make mistakes. Carry God's blessing with pride and remember why Jesus died." Her words felt like a lifeline, reminding me of God's sovereignty and love. That day freed me from months of shame and planted the seeds of confidence that God's plans are higher than mine.

Reflecting today, I thank God for my now thirty-eight-year-old son, a testimony of His goodness. I thank Jesus for leading me from embarrassment to gratitude, for providing for me, and for allowing me to thrive in ways I never imagined. I never lacked—not once. When you accept God's unconditional love and His plan, and your fully grasp His anointing, you can walk free of any shame or embarrassment.

## Scriptural Reflection:
*2 Timothy 1:8 (NRSV)*: "Do not be ashamed, then, of the testimony about our Lord . . . but join with me in suffering for the gospel, relying on the power of God."

## Spiritual Reflection:
The Samaritan woman at the well (*John 4:1-26*) experienced shame and societal rejection, yet Jesus met her in her moment of need, extending love and revealing His identity. Her life was transformed, and she went on to share her testimony with others.

## Self-Reflection Question:
Is there an area in your life where guilt or fear of embarrassment is holding you back from fully accepting God's love and purpose? How might you invite Him to help you walk in freedom today?

**Reflection Prayer:**
Lord, thank You for Your love that covers all shame. Help me to see myself as You see me, walking in the freedom You offer. Let my life be a testimony of Your grace, and may I embrace Your plan with confidence. Amen.

# Pause. Breathe.
# Write what is on your heart.

# You Don't Know My Prayers

For years, we've echoed the phrase, "You don't know my story." It's been a cultural anthem—offering space for empathy, healing, and at times, validation. But have you ever paused to consider the weight of that phrase?

Stories, after all, are interpretations—they can be embellished or edited, inspire sympathy or trigger sorrow, nurture dysfunction or glorify trauma. A story can highlight the event, but not always the encounter.

But when I say, "You don't know my prayers," I'm not offering a rewritten tale—I'm testifying to something sacred and unseen. When I pray, I'm calling on Elohim, the Creator of heaven and earth, who answers according to His perfect will. I'm leaning on El Roi, the God who sees me in the valley, the desert, and the silence. I trust El Chay, the Living God, who breathes fresh answers into what man thought was finished.

You may think you know my story, but you don't know my prayers—those intimate moments whispered through clenched teeth and tear-stained pillows, the silent ones cried between breaths, or the declarations screamed from a soul refusing to give up.

Throughout Scripture, it wasn't the story that moved mountains—it was the prayer born out of the story.

## Scriptural Reflection:

Psalm 34:6 (NIV): "This poor man cried, and the Lord heard him, and saved him out of all his troubles." (*This verse reminds us that while people may know what happened to us, only God hears the raw, unfiltered prayers that rise from our deepest places.*)

## Spiritual Reflection:

In 1 Samuel 1, we meet Hannah, a woman mired in the bitterness of barrenness. Her story was one of sorrow, ridicule, and longing—but it was her prayer that shifted the heavens. She poured out her soul before the Lord, and in return, He gifted her with Samuel—a prophet, priest, and judge. Her story was real, but it was her prayer that was powerful.

## Self-Reflection Question:

If someone only knew your story, what part of your truth would be missing because they never heard your prayers?

## Reflection Prayer:

El Roi, you see the pain behind our smiles, the heaviness behind our strength, and the prayers behind our stories. Today, we release every narrative we've written in our minds and exchange it for Your promises. Remind us that even when our stories are messy, our prayers are heard. Strengthen us to pray with boldness, to believe with expectancy, and trust with courage. May we live not by the limitations of our story but by the liberation of our prayers. In Jesus' name, amen.

**Pause. Breathe.
Write what is on your heart.**

# It Will Pass

As I reflect on my journey, I must be honest—life has not always been kind. I've walked through seasons where the attacks felt relentless, like waves crashing one after another with no chance to catch my breath. Just when I thought I was standing strong, life would throw another blow. "If it ain't one thing, it's another" became my weary, whispered anthem. I often wondered, *Am I being punished? Why does life keep targeting me? What did I do to deserve this?*

In my lowest moments, escape seemed easier than endurance. The weight of trial after trial had me convinced that relief was nowhere in sight. But I've come to understand something vital—pressure has purpose.

Imagine a pressure cooker. Inside, the contents are subjected to intense heat. The pressure tenderizes, transforms, and prepares the food to nourish. But if that pressure is released too early, the food remains undercooked, unfit, and unready.

The same is true for us. We are being prepared, molded, strengthened. If we run before the process is complete, we emerge underdeveloped, wounded, and unable to pour into others.

Pressure can feel like wandering in the wilderness—hungry for hope, stripped of joy, uncertain of direction. But even wilderness seasons have an expiration date. *This will pass.* The suffering, the confusion, the doubt—they don't last forever. They're temporary chapters in a greater story.

God is not absent in the fire. He's with us in the trial—working through the trial and building something afterward. The same God who created the heavens knows your name. He sees you. He strengthens you. He walks with you.

King David understood this truth. Though he was anointed, he still endured betrayal, loneliness, hiding in caves, and fleeing from those who wanted him dead. But in the midst of it all, David held onto hope, declaring, "The Lord is my strength and my shield; my heart trusts in Him, and He helps me" (Psalm 28:7, NIV).

David knew what many of us forget when the storm hits: God's presence doesn't prevent the fire—it preserves you through it.

God never wastes pain, so don't despise the process and don't fear the pressure. Every tear, every setback, and every delay will produce something far more valuable than comfort—character, faith, and purpose.

## Scriptural Reflection:

1 Peter 5:10 (ESV): "And after you have suffered a little while, the God of all grace, who has called you to His eternal glory in Christ, will Himself restore, confirm, strengthen, and establish you."

## Spiritual Reflection:

Consider Joseph, the dreamer. He was betrayed by his own brothers, sold into slavery, falsely accused, imprisoned, and forgotten. For years, it seemed like one setback after another. But in every dark season, God was setting Joseph up for something greater. When the time was right—when the pressure had produced maturity, wisdom, and humility—Joseph was elevated to a position of influence that not only saved nations but also reconciled him with his family.

Joseph's story teaches us that what sometimes feels like delay is often divine development. The pit, the prison, and the pressure were all preparation for the palace.

## Self-Reflection Question:

Can I recognize ways that God has preserved, matured, or strengthened me through past pressures? What might God be preparing me for in this current season?

### Reflection Prayer:

Father, I trust You in the midst of this struggle. Help me to endure and to trust that this season will pass. Give me the strength to grow, knowing You are with me always. Grant me understanding that this too shall pass, and when it does, I'll rise stronger, wiser, and better equipped to help others through their valley. Amen.

**Pause. Breathe.
Write what is on your heart.**

# That's Not My Story

How many times have you opened up—heart bare and honest—sharing your deepest valleys, your hardest lessons, and your greatest triumphs with someone you trusted . . . only to later hear your story retold in a way that felt foreign, fragmented, and falsely framed?

It's a crushing feeling. You sit in stunned silence thinking, "That's not my story."

And you're absolutely right—it's not.

Too often, people speak on our behalf without our permission. They take pieces of what they think they know and stitch together a version of events that fits their narrative. But they don't know the full weight of the battles you've fought. They didn't sit with you in the quiet hours when God mended your broken spirit. They didn't hear the silent prayers, the cries that had no words. They didn't witness the real process—just the headlines they created in their own minds.

And let's be honest—many times these retellings are rooted in jealousy, envy, or insecurity. It's easier for some to try to reduce your testimony than confront what your resilience reveals about their own lack of healing. They can't quite grasp what they see in you—strength, grace, favor, anointing—so they minimize it. But here's what you must remember—they didn't write your story, so they don't get to narrate it.

You are the full, uncut testimony of God's goodness, not the edited version they present. Your story is sacred—penned by the hand of the Almighty. It includes pain, yes, but also purpose. It carries scars, but also strength. And no one can tell it quite like you, because no one lived it like you did. You were there when the storm broke—and you were there when God calmed it. You were there when it all fell apart—and you were there when He picked up every shattered piece.

So the next time someone tries to define you by a distorted version of your truth, lift your head, speak boldly, and say it out loud if you must—"That's not my story." And then walk in the truth of who you are --- and Whose you are.

You don't have to chase every false narrative. Let your life, your healing, and your peace be the evidence. God knows the real story—and He's still writing it.

## Scriptural Reflection:
Exodus 14:14 (NIV): "The Lord will fight for you; you need only to be still."

## Spiritual Reflection:
Consider Joseph, whose brothers distorted his story out of jealousy. They didn't understand God's plan for his life and saw him as a threat. Yet, in the end, Joseph's story wasn't defined by their intentions but by God's purpose. As Joseph said, "You intended to harm me, but God intended it for good to accomplish what is now being done, the saving of many lives" (Genesis 50:20).

God will use your story in the same way—regardless of how others twist it—to reveal His love and truth to others. He reigns supreme over every chapter, and we don't need to waste energy defending our story against misinterpretations. Trust that the true Author of your life knows how to use every page, every word, for His glory and your good.

## Self-Reflection Question:
What part of your story feels misunderstood or misrepresented by others? How can you invite God to help you release the need to "correct" it and instead trust Him with the narrative He is writing through you?

### Reflection Prayer:

Lord, help me trust You as the true Author of my story. Teach me to let go of the need to control how others perceive me and remind me that You alone define my worth. May my life reflect Your purpose and grace, no matter how it's retold by others. Amen.

**Pause. Breathe.
Write what is on your heart.**

# I'm Courageous, Not Crazy

Have you ever noticed how people sometimes mistake your boldness for recklessness, your vision for wildness? When you step out in ways that others wouldn't dare, they might call you "over the top." But you're not "crazy"—you're courageous! You were fearfully and wonderfully made (Psalm 139:14), and your Creator didn't design you to fit into the usual mold.

You don't think the way everyone else does because God gave you a unique purpose. And as you dare to live that purpose, remember that "With God, all things are possible" (Matthew 19:26). What some call "crazy," others will recognize as faith, determination, and trust in the God who goes before you.

When you know the One who conquered all, you can rest assured that no challenge can overcome you and no obstacle can weaken you. God holds the plans for your life, and in His promise, "No weapon formed against you shall prosper" (Isaiah 54:17). Yes, difficulties will arise—they're part of the journey, keeping us grounded and aligned with His will—but don't let them discourage you. God uses them to strengthen and humble you.

So be bold. Stand tall. Show the courage that He's placed within you. Because with Him, you're not just fearless—you're unshakable.

## Scriptural Reflection:

Joshua 1:9 (NIV): "Have I not commanded you? Be strong and courageous. Do not be afraid; do not be discouraged, for the Lord your God will be with you wherever you go."

## Spiritual Reflection:

David and Goliath (*1 Samuel 17*) – When David faced Goliath, others saw a young, inexperienced shepherd boy going up against an undefeatable giant. But David knew his courage wasn't crazy—it was grounded in God's power. By believing in God's strength over his own, he became victorious in what seemed like an impossible battle.

## Self-Reflection Question:

Where have I held back from stepping out in faith because of fear or the opinions of others? How would my life change if I truly believed that God's strength and protection go with me?

### Reflection Prayer:

Lord, give me the courage to move forward boldly, trusting that You walk with me. Let my faith be bigger than my fear, and may my actions show Your strength in me. Lead me with clarity and help me see challenges as part of Your plan to shape me. Amen.

**Pause. Breathe.
Write what is on your heart.**

# Circle It

There's power in drawing circles around our Reflection Prayers—a bold act of faith that claims God's promises and seeks His will with intention. This practice became life-changing for me during a season when I felt weary, worn out, and anxious, particularly about an upcoming exam. Mark Batterson's insights on praying hard and bold in *The Circle Maker* were the encouragement I didn't know I needed.

At that time, anxiety was weighing heavily on me. I was scheduled to take my counseling exam for the second time, and fear seemed to have anchored itself to me. I'm not a natural test-taker—I can study intensely and understand a topic well, but when the test is right in front of me, it feels like every bit of knowledge evaporates. Desperate, I felt led to do something symbolic and powerful—I created a Reflection Prayer circle with ribbons and even went out to buy a hula hoop. I'd step inside, placing myself and my Reflection Prayers within the circle, seeking strength, wisdom, and God's presence as I studied and prepared.

It was within this circle that God revealed something new to me. I had believed counseling was my calling, but through these moments of Reflection Prayer, the Holy Spirit shifted my perspective. I realized that my true purpose was not just to counsel but to coach people through life. God was inviting me on a journey to guide others in finding their path, bringing encouragement and direction to those seeking purpose and growth.

Consider how God sometimes redirects us toward a purpose greater than we had imagined. Embrace His plans, knowing they are rooted in love and lead to hope.

Thank You, Jesus, for using that circle to redefine my path and empower me to step into what You had in store all along.

## Scriptural Reflection:
Proverbs 16:9 (NIV): "In their hearts humans plan their course, but the Lord establishes their steps."

## Spiritual Reflection:
Reflect on Joshua, who was called not only to lead Israel but also to enter and conquer the Promised Land. Joshua's courage came from a bold dependence on God, and through every challenge, he circled back to the promise that God would be with him. Joshua's leadership wasn't just about his strengths—it was about a deep, faith-filled response to God's calling.

### Self-Reflection Question:

As you pray and seek God's direction, are you open to the possibility that He may reveal a purpose different from what you've planned? How might you respond if He calls you to something new?

### Reflection Prayer for Courage:

Lord, grant me the courage to follow Your guidance and the strength to step boldly into new purposes. Help me trust Your plans and be open to Your direction, knowing that You will empower me every step of the way. Amen.

**Pause. Breathe.
Write what is on your heart.**

# Choosing Kindness

I've often tried to model kindness for others, but I realized that I never fully grasped its importance in my own life—especially at work. I felt that if I didn't learn things instantly, I'd be seen as incompetent. I wanted control—of the outcomes, the perceptions, and the narrative.

As age refines my mind, it allows me the opportunity to take nothing for granted. I've learned to bask in the moment with thankfulness and gratitude, realizing that God owes me nothing, and everything He entrusts to me is due to His kindness and compassion.

Every kind act that God bestows upon me should be reciprocated to others. His love is never meant to stop with me—it flows through me, creating a ripple effect of grace, mercy, and encouragement.

If we're honest, there are times we don't feel like being kind. Unkind energy from others can influence us, making us question our own character. But kindness is more than a reaction—it's a strength rooted in self-control and genuine love, even in situations we can't control. Today, I'm choosing kindness for myself as much as for others. When we act with kindness, we tap into a deeper love, care, and support that only grows stronger with use.

Kindness is not just an action—it's a reflection of God's presence within us. It has the power to soften hardened hearts, heal unseen wounds, and restore hope in places where it has faded. Every time we choose kindness, we mirror God's grace and demonstrate His light in a world that can often feel dark. So let's not grow weary of doing good. Instead, let kindness become our default—an unshakable part of who we are—knowing that each small act plants seeds of faith and love that will bloom in due time.

## Scriptural Reflection:

Ephesians 4:32 (NIV): "Be kind and compassionate to one another, forgiving each other, just as in Christ God forgave you."

## Spiritual Reflection:

Think of Ruth, who demonstrated kindness to Naomi despite their shared hardships. She chose to stay and support Naomi when she could have left, showing us that true kindness is sacrificial and enduring. In the same way, our kindness shouldn't be dependent on convenience but on conviction, as even the smallest act of love can lead to transformation.

## Self-Reflection Question:

Where in your life could you extend kindness, even if it's challenging, and what might that change in your relationships with others and yourself?

## Reflection Prayer:

Lord, help me to show kindness as Jesus did, with genuine love and compassion. Let Your strength be my foundation so that kindness becomes my natural response, even in difficult situations. Amen.

Pause. Breathe.
Write what is on your heart.

# You Can Soar!

When I think of interviews, I often recall the S.O.A.R. format: Situation, Obstacle, Action, and Result—a structured way to tell a story. But life doesn't always follow a script. The situations and obstacles we face aren't neatly packaged, and sometimes we stay stuck where we don't belong.

I've experienced this firsthand—pursuing what I wanted instead of what God intended. I've lingered in jobs, relationships, and even ministries that were never meant to be my landing place. Instead of moving forward, I settled. Stagnated.

Too often, we cling to habits, environments, or mindsets that hinder our growth. We hold on to comfort, even when it keeps us in a downward spiral. But you can't SOAR in a dead place. True elevation requires release—letting go of excuses, breaking free from selfish desires, and aligning with God's will. Only then can we rise above dysfunction, past wounds, and learned behaviors.

God always provides a way of escape and the opportunity to soar. Spiritually, to soar means to rise above—not by our own strength but by His divine purpose. To soar like an eagle requires patience, focus, and faith in the unseen winds of God's plan.

## Scriptural Reflection:

Isaiah 40:31 (NIV): "But those who hope in the Lord will renew their strength. They will soar on wings like eagles; they will run and not grow weary; they will walk and not be faint."

## Spiritual Reflection:

Consider Moses—a man who battled self-doubt, opposition, and overwhelming obstacles. Yet God lifted him above his limitations, transforming him into the leader of His people. Moses didn't just endure—he soared.

## Self-Reflection Question:

Where might God be calling you to rise above your current obstacles? Beyond just surviving, what would soaring look like in your life?

### Reflection Prayer:

Lord, lift me above my challenges. Help me to fully trust in You so I may soar beyond every obstacle with purpose, clarity, and faith. Amen.

**Pause. Breathe.
Write what is on your heart.**

# Stop Apologizing For Your Uniqueness

As a motivational life coach, one of my favorite questions to have clients ask themselves is, "Who am I?" It's a simple question, yet powerful enough to shake the very foundations of how we perceive ourselves. When we strip away the titles—mom, dad, son, daughter, husband, wife—and roles like manager, educator, or entrepreneur, we are left with the raw, authentic essence of who we truly are.

This journey of self-discovery isn't just empowering—it's essential. Understanding our unique identity allows us to see how intentionally and intricately we were designed.

If I had to answer that question for myself, I'd say, "I am bold, confident, uniquely crafted, fearless, and faithful." These words aren't just affirmations—they're reflections of the divine fingerprint God placed on my life.

But here's the truth—the world will sometimes try to diminish your light. People may misunderstand, criticize, or label you as "too much" or "not enough." Yet the One who created you never intended for you to shrink or conform. You are a one-of-a-kind masterpiece. God didn't design you to be a carbon copy of anyone else.

When I look in the mirror, I choose to see God's artistry—and I refuse to apologize for who I am. And neither should you. Embrace every part of the person God handcrafted with purpose and love.

So today, stand firm. Be unshaken by the opinions of others. Celebrate your uniqueness—God Himself has called you worthy, valued, and deeply loved.

You are not a mistake. You are a *miracle*.

## Scriptural Reflection:

Psalm 139:14 (NIV) says, "I am fearfully and wonderfully made." This is our truth. God saw fit to make us as we are, each aspect carefully molded by His hand.

## Spiritual Reflection:

Take Esther, for example. She was a young Jewish woman thrust into a royal position in a foreign land. She could have hidden her heritage, shrunk back, or apologized for being different. But instead, she rose in courage and declared her uniqueness when it mattered most. Her boldness not only saved her people but affirmed that she was placed in that moment "for such a time as this" (Esther 4:14).

## Self-Reflection Question:

What would change in your life if you stopped apologizing for who God created you to be? How would it feel to walk confidently in your unique gifts and personality without seeking validation from others?

## Reflection Prayer:

Lord, thank You for the masterpiece You've created in me. Help me to stand confidently in my identity, embracing my unique beauty, strengths, and calling. May I honor You by living unapologetically, reflecting Your love and grace each day. Amen.

# Pause. Breathe.
# Write what is on your heart.

# Activate Your Trust, Then Wait Patiently

Have you ever found yourself overstaying in a season—worn out from waiting and frustrated with the delay? I know I have. Maybe it was for a job promotion, a change in your relationship status, a financial breakthrough, or a medical cure. The wait made you impatient, anxious, and desperate for change. You tried to force an outcome, but in doing so, you set the clock back and started the wait all over again.

My experience was one of longing for freedom. I was handed the keys to a new house and entered a life with a man I wasn't married to. Deep down, I knew it wasn't in line with God's plan for me. Each night, I struggled, crying myself to sleep, unhappy with my choices. One day, during a women's study group, I was given a journal with 1 Corinthians 10:13 inside: "No temptation has overtaken you except what is common to mankind. And God is faithful; he will not let you be tempted beyond what you can bear. But when you are tempted, he will also provide a way out so that you can endure it."

That verse hit me—it showed me that God understood my heart. I saw my reflection, and God spoke to me: *"I got you."* Soon after, He proved it—by placing in my hand the keys to my own home.

Don't rush the wait. When you feel overwhelmed by circumstances or tempted to escape by your own means, lean into God's guidance. Trust Him with your wait and let Him lead you toward what He has planned.

## Scriptural Reflection:
Psalm 27:14 (NIV): "Wait for the Lord; be strong and take heart and wait for the Lord."

## Spiritual Reflection:
Think of Joseph, who had dreams of greatness but waited through years of slavery, imprisonment, and injustice before God's promise was fulfilled. Joseph's life shows us that waiting with faith—even through hardship—prepares us for greater blessings than we could imagine.

## Self-Reflection Question:
Am I trying to control my circumstances to end my wait, or am I allowing God to guide me patiently toward His perfect timing?

## Reflection Prayer:

Lord, help me trust You in my waiting. Teach me to be patient and to find peace in Your timing. Strengthen my heart to rely on You, knowing that You have a plan for my good. Amen.

**Pause. Breathe.
Write what is on your heart.**

# Father or Daddy?

Growing up, I never called anyone "daddy." That word didn't exist in my experience. The man who biologically held that title was absent. But in his place stood my granddaddy—a steady, loving presence who quietly taught me what care, consistency, and protection looked like. Still, the word "daddy" never felt like mine to use.

That's probably why I always found it difficult when people referred to God as "daddy." To me, God was majestic, holy, sovereign—Elohim, El Shaddai, El Roi, Abba Father. "Daddy" felt too soft, too casual, too common for the Creator of heaven and earth. But as I've grown spiritually, I've begun to realize that maybe it's not about the word—it's about the relationship.

Some say "daddy" because they've encountered God as the ever-present, gentle, guiding hand—the loving parent they can run to without fear. I didn't start there, but now I see that God wants to be known in both majesty and intimacy. He's not just our Father in heaven—He's the One who draws close enough to wipe our tears, calm our fears, and walk with us through the mess.

That word *Abba*—Aramaic for "Father" or "Daddy"—carries both reverence and intimacy. It's what Jesus Himself cried out in Gethsemane (Mark 14:36), a term of both trust and deep dependence.

Jesus shows us that calling God *Abba*—like saying "Daddy"—isn't childish. It's the language of surrender, of trust, of knowing you're held even when everything around you feels uncertain.

Remember, your language doesn't have to match others, but your relationship with God should reflect honesty, growth, and closeness. If "Daddy" still feels distant, start by leaning into *Abba*—the bridge between holiness and heart.

## Scriptural Reflection:

Romans 8:15 (NLT): "So you have not received a spirit that makes you fearful slaves. Instead, you received God's Spirit when he adopted you as his own children. Now we call him, 'Abba, Father.'"

## Spiritual Reflection:

Jesus in the Garden: In Gethsemane, Jesus faced overwhelming sorrow and distress. In His moment of deepest need, He didn't cry out with formality—He cried out with familiarity: "Abba, Father, everything is possible for you. Take this cup from me. Yet not what I will, but what you will" (Mark 14:36).

## Self-Reflection Questions:

What title do you most often use for God—and what does that reveal about how you see Him? Are you holding back intimacy with God because of your earthly experiences with father figures?

## Reflection Prayer:

Abba Father, thank You for meeting me where words fall short. You are holy and near, sovereign and tender. Help me to know You beyond titles and embrace the relationship You offer. Heal the broken pieces of my father story so I can receive You fully. In Jesus' name, amen.

**Pause. Breathe.
Write what is on your heart.**

# Serving an Uncommon God

We spend much of our lives in the realm of the common—common routines, common decisions, and even common expectations. We operate in the common so often that we often take the uncommon for granted. Our mindset is often shaped by what we call "common sense." But is it really common sense to believe a check could show up in your mailbox out of nowhere? Sounds unlikely, even *uncommon*, doesn't it?

Have you ever tried to achieve the impossible using common methods? Maybe you've longed for financial freedom, so you pursued get-rich-quick schemes or bought stacks of lottery tickets, hoping for a breakthrough. But deep down, you know those strategies won't unlock the extraordinary life you desire.

Here's the truth: The key to a life of uncommon blessings isn't found in shortcuts or human efforts—it's found in a genuine, unwavering relationship with God through Jesus Christ. It requires us to shift from a casual, doubtful mindset to a bold, faith-filled posture that trusts God to be exactly who He has promised to be.

We serve an uncommon God. His ways defy logic, His power has no limits, and His plans exceed imagination. Through Him, we have access to supernatural provision, divine favor, and miracles beyond human comprehension. But there's a catch—this life requires obedience. Yes, obedience! When we trust and obey an uncommon God, we open the door to an overflow of blessings, protection, and purpose.

So today, don't waste your grace living a common life when you serve an uncommon God.

## Scriptural Reflection:

Isaiah 55:8-9 (NIV): "For My thoughts are not your thoughts, neither are your ways My ways," declares the Lord. "As the heavens are higher than the earth, so are My ways higher than your ways and My thoughts than your thoughts."

## Spiritual Reflection:

Noah was a man who embraced the uncommon nature of God. In a world full of corruption and wickedness, God gave Noah an extraordinary command—to build an ark in preparation for a flood that had never been seen before. Despite the ridicule from those around him,

Noah obeyed. His faith in an uncommon God allowed him to fulfill an extraordinary purpose (Genesis 6).

## Self-Reflection Questions:

Are there areas in your life where you've limited God to what seems "common" or possible by human standards? What is one step of faith you can take today to trust God's uncommon purpose for your life?

## Reflection Prayer:

Lord, You are uncommon in every way. Help me to trust Your plans and step beyond ordinary boundaries. Strengthen my faith to align my heart with Your extraordinary will. In Jesus' name, amen.

**Pause. Breathe.
Write what is on your heart.**

# Seasons of the Unexpected: Finding Purpose in Pain

Life has a way of throwing us into unexpected and often uncomfortable seasons. These seasons come in various forms—illness, the loss of a loved one, betrayal, or even the unraveling of a dream we once held dear. My unexpected season came in the form of a divorce.

I entered marriage believing in the sacredness of "till death do us part." When my marriage fell apart, I was left devastated, hurt, and questioning everything. Why me? How could this happen? I felt betrayed, hopeless, and like a complete failure.

One evening, during a church revival, the pastor posed a question that hit my core: "How do you know the person you're with is the person God had for you?" I had no answer. I realized I'd never sought God about the marriage before saying "I do." Over time, I understood the truth—my union had not been God's design for my life.

For years, I wrestled with that reality, staying in a situation God had already released me from. But during that season, I learned something profound—God never abandons us in our pain. He sees the end from the beginning (Isaiah 46:10), and His plans for us are always good, even when our circumstances are not (Jeremiah 29:11).

## Scriptural Reflection:

James 1:2-4 (NIV): "Consider it pure joy, my brothers and sisters, whenever you face trials of many kinds, because you know that the testing of your faith produces perseverance. Let perseverance finish its work so that you may be mature and complete, not lacking anything."

## Spiritual Reflection:

The unexpected seasons of life are not meant to destroy us but to refine us. Consider Joseph, who endured betrayal, false accusations, and imprisonment. What seemed like a series of devastating setbacks was God's way of positioning him to save an entire nation (Genesis 50:20). In the same way, God uses our pain to shape our purpose.

## Self-Reflection Question:

Are you clinging to something God may be asking you to release? How might trusting His plan over your expectations bring peace to your heart in this season?

## Reflection Prayer:

Heavenly Father, in seasons of uncertainty and pain, remind me that You are my refuge and strength. Help me trust Your plans and release what no longer serves Your purpose. Teach me to see Your hand, even in the unexpected. Guide me into the peace that surpasses all understanding. In Jesus' name, amen.

**Pause. Breathe.
Write what is on your heart.**

# Don't Starve Your Spirit — Feed Your Soul Daily

For years, I leaned on others for my spiritual growth outside of church. I was thirsty for God's Word and thought that well-structured Christians could pour it into me. I found myself constantly waiting on others to feed my spirit—sharing what they read, prayed, or learned. I was used to saying, "Please pray for me," not realizing that while asking for prayer is okay, I needed to shift my posture and start asking, "Please pray with me."

I thought simply being connected to mature Christian saints was enough to help me overcome life's challenges and unforeseen obstacles because, in my mind, they had it all together. Reality check? They didn't. Many were drowning in spiritual tenure but lacked true faith. They were teaching from personal experiences and carnal lessons learned, not from a place of surrender to God's Word. The truth? Unlike them, I wasn't drowning—I was thirsty, not dehydrated.

Your body can't fully function when you're dehydrated—you need water to replenish and restore you. But thirst is a reminder that something is missing, that you need nourishment before it becomes a crisis. I hadn't lost myself enough to crave that pure sprinkle of water—the fountain of living water only God provides. Spiritual dehydration had left me depleted and far from God's presence. Honestly, I hadn't surrendered fully to Him. My spirit was thirsting for the life-giving water He offers.

That wake-up call changed everything. I realized I couldn't keep waiting for someone else to feed me. My spirit was starving, and I was draining those around me—and you can't rely on a near-dry well to quench your thirst. That's when I became intentional and invested in my spiritual growth—purchasing books, study Bibles, and tools to dive deeper into God's Word. It wasn't up to my pastor, a prophet, or a priest to do it for me. It was up to me to seek Him daily.

Thank You, Jesus, for my season of thirst that led me to the fountain of life. I now understand that neglecting God's Word is not an option, and feeding my spirit isn't a once-a-week event—it's a daily necessity.

### Scriptural Reflection:

John 4:14 (NIV): "But whoever drinks the water I give them will never thirst. Indeed, the water I give them will become in them a spring of water welling up to eternal life."

## Spiritual Reflection:

I'm reminded of the Samaritan woman at the well (John 4:7–26). She came searching for physical water but had a deeper spiritual thirst she couldn't articulate. She had tried to fill the void in her life with relationships, approval, and routine, but none of it satisfied her soul. Jesus met her in her dry place and offered her "living water"—a source that would never run dry.

## Self-Reflection Question:

Are you spiritually thirsty? Are you waiting for someone to feed you, or are you willing to take that step toward God's living water?

## Reflection Prayer:

Lord, help me recognize the thirst in my soul as a call to draw closer to You. Fill my heart with Your truth and my spirit with Your strength. Help me crave Your Word as nourishment for my soul. Teach me to seek Your living water daily and to rely fully on Your Word for nourishment. In Jesus' name, amen.

Pause. Breathe.
Write what's on your heart.

# Life's Chaos, God's Control

Our generation has a way with words, and one of my favorite phrases is, "Life is lifing." It perfectly captures those seasons when life feels like an unrelenting roller coaster—twists, turns, trials, and disappointments hitting all at once. The pressure piles on, and it feels like every exit sign has suddenly disappeared, leaving us stranded in a maze of stress, setbacks, and heartache.

Here's a reality check—life *is* lifing right now. The world around us is shifting at an exhausting pace. It's chaotic, unpredictable, and downright discouraging at times. People are losing jobs, homes, savings, and their sense of security. Many are being forced into survival mode, having to make tough decisions with little time to prepare. Conversations seem to start with the same anxious questions. What is happening? How are we going to make it? What should we do next? These questions stem from a fear of the unknown.

But as I sit with this phrase, another question stirs in my spirit—if life is lifing, is God God'ing? In other words, is the God of the universe still sovereign? Still loving? Still present in the midst of all this chaos, constant change, and questionable leadership? Is He surprised by our burdens, or has He already provided a way to navigate them?

The truth is, God is still on the throne. He's still moving, still working, still GOD'ing over every circumstance. He holds authority over all things and all people. No worldly upheaval can dethrone Him.

## Scriptural Reflection:

Romans 8:28 (NIV): "And we know that in all things God works for the good of those who love Him, who have been called according to His purpose."

## Spiritual Reflection:

The story of Joseph offers a powerful reminder of this truth. Joseph's life was filled with hardship—betrayed by his own brothers, sold into slavery, falsely accused, and thrown into prison—but through it all, God was working behind the scenes, orchestrating a plan for his good and the good of many. Joseph later declared in Genesis 50:20, "You intended to harm me, but God intended it for good to accomplish what is now being done, the saving of many lives."

If God could bring beauty from Joseph's ashes, imagine what He can do in your life. The key is trusting Him—even when you can't see the end of the road.

## Self-Reflection Question:

How would your mindset and decisions shift if you truly believed that God is working for your good, even when life feels unbearable?

## Reflection Prayer:

Lord, when life feels overwhelming, remind me that You are in control. Help me trust Your plans, even when I don't understand them. Strengthen my faith, guide my steps, and lighten my burdens. Thank You for being my ever-present help in trouble. In You, I find peace, purpose, and hope. In Jesus' name, amen.

## Pause. Breathe.
## Write what is on your heart.

# All Is Not Lost

As you sit with your thoughts today, take a moment to reflect. Despite how things may look, could it possibly be worse? The fact that you're breathing, your heart is pumping, and your mind is actively processing this moment is evidence that all is not lost.

I know this because I've lived it. After twenty-one years in a job that offered security, stability, and a steady six-figure paycheck, I walked away. I left not out of fear or failure—but because of faith. For years, I prayed the same prayer: "Lord, let me retire." I repeated it over and over, expecting it to unfold my way, in my timing, with my plan. But God heard me.

He answered—but not the way my limited sight or finite mind had imagined. He made a way that only He could design. And now, even as I step into the unknown, I say, with a heart full of gratitude, "Thank You, Jesus."

I don't know exactly what life will look like in this next chapter of "retirement," but I do know this—God has me covered. The six-figure paycheck may no longer hit my account, but my SOURCE—Jehovah Jireh—has resources far greater than anything I could ever imagine. All is not lost.

Consider Job, who lost everything—wealth, family, health—but still declared, "Though He slay me, yet will I trust Him." God restored Job and honored his faith. And just like Job, I believe restoration is on the way for me—and for you too.

## Scriptural Reflection:
Lamentations 3:22-23 (NIV): also, Lord never ceases; his mercies never come to an end; they are new every morning; great is Your faithfulness."

## Spiritual Reflection:
Like the story of Naomi—what seemed lost was actually being repositioned. Naomi's story in Ruth is one of deep loss—she lost her husband, her sons, her sense of home, and even her sense of identity. She renamed herself *Mara*, meaning "bitter," because she felt God had turned against her. But even in her grief, God was at work behind the scenes. Through Ruth's loyalty, Boaz's kindness, and divine timing, Noami's emptiness was filled. Her lineage would ultimately connect to King David—and to Jesus.

## Self-Reflection Question:

What prayers have you prayed over and over that God may have already answered—just not in the way you expected? Can you trust His method even when it doesn't match your plan?

## Reflection Prayer:

Lord, thank You for hearing the prayers I've whispered for years. Help me trust Your way, even when it looks different than mine. I know You are faithful. Amen

**Pause. Breathe.
Write what is on your heart.**

# Remove: Letting Go of What Hinders

"A time to search and a time to give up, a time to keep and a time to throw away." —*Ecclesiastes 3:6 (NIV)*

Let's be honest—too often we stay connected to things long past their expiration date. We live as if every connection must be permanent, even when we know deep down the "situational-ship" is toxic, draining, or simply not aligned with who God has called us to be.

We cling because it's comfortable and once brought fulfillment, joy, or meaning—but now it's just weight. And still, we hold on. Perhaps it's a fear of embarrassment, judgment, or failure. Maybe it's the voices of naysayers echoing louder than God's whisper of purpose. Or it could simply be a fear of change.

Let me repeat this truth, even if I've mentioned it elsewhere, because sometimes it takes hearing something twenty million times before it finally lands in our hearts. And if that's what it takes for your freedom, then let's say it again and again: *You cannot heal while still holding on to what's hurting you.*

Ask yourself what you've missed out on by holding onto something that is burying you alive. That relationship. That habit. That false security. That mindset. You may have convinced yourself it was manageable, even necessary—but God's been calling you to release it. Because what you won't remove can rot your faith from the inside out.

## Scriptural Reflection

Matthew 15:13 (NIV): "Every plant that My heavenly Father has not planted will be pulled up by the roots." Sometimes the root must be removed—not just trimmed. Let God pull it up completely.

## Spiritual Reflection

Letting go starts with acknowledging what no longer aligns with God's will. It's praying, "Lord, show me what You see. Remove what no longer belongs."

Look at Jonah. God called him to Nineveh—but Jonah had other plans. He ran. He resisted. He clung to his will instead of surrendering to God's. But in His mercy, God allowed a storm—and a fish—to interrupt Jonah's rebellion and reroute him toward purpose. It wasn't comfortable. It wasn't pretty. But it was necessary.

Just like Jonah, your removal process might feel painful—but it's packed with purpose.

## Self-Reflection Question
What are you holding on to that God is trying to remove? What part of your life feels like it's keeping you hostage when God is calling you higher?

## Reflection Prayer:
Heavenly Father,

Today I give You permission to prune my life. Remove what hinders, even if it hurts. Pull up every root that's not of You. Help me release every person, place, thought, or pattern that no longer aligns with Your will for my life. I want to trust You more than I trust my comfort zone. Give me the courage to surrender what I cannot fix and the faith to believe that what You have ahead is greater than anything I leave behind. In Jesus' name, amen.

# Pause. Breathe.
# Write what is on your heart.

# Reboot: A Fresh Start in the Spirit

Have you ever felt like your soul was stuck on a loading screen—spinning, lagging, unable to move forward? That's your spiritual system signaling it's time for a reboot.

A spiritual reboot isn't just a pause—it's a bold, divine refresh. It's when you intentionally invite God to realign your heart and mind with His truth. It's about shutting down the background noise of doubt, fear, insecurity, and complacency and tuning into the only voice that matters—God's.

Are you ready? Are you ready to stop scripting your own version of the story and surrender the pen to the Author of Life? Are you ready to break free from the need to fit in and finally walk in what God has set apart for you? Are you done copying the world's template and prepared to embrace heaven's blueprint? If you whispered yes—then it's time. Click the reset button. Go ahead—God is waiting.

God is your pen and your paper. He's already written your story. Your steps are ordered. Your destiny is prepared.

Just as we reboot our devices to clear out corrupted files and fix lagging performance, we must regularly reset our lives. Why? Because distractions creep in. Doubt sneaks up. Our connection with God can weaken in the static of daily life. Rebooting resets your spiritual flow, reestablishes your focus, and recharges your faith.

### Scriptural Reflection:

Romans 12:2 (NIV): "Do not conform to the pattern of this world, but be transformed by the renewing of your mind. Then you will be able to test and approve what God's will is—His good, pleasing and perfect will."

### Spiritual Reflection:

Rebooting spiritually is an act of surrender. It's saying, "God, I trust You more than I trust my own timeline, plan, or comfort zone." It's choosing divine alignment over personal ambition. When your spirit is refreshed and your mind renewed, you begin to hear clearly, see differently, and walk boldly in purpose.

Think of Saul's transformation into Paul. Saul was on a mission of destruction—persecuting Christians with passion and authority. But on the road to Damascus,

God hit the ultimate reset button. With one encounter, Saul was blinded—physically and spiritually—and in that darkness, God rebooted his entire identity. He became Paul—bold apostle, kingdom builder, and purpose-driven man on fire for Christ.

Paul's story reminds us that no matter how far off course we may have drifted, one divine encounter can reroute our entire life.

## Self-Reflection Questions:

In what areas have I been trying to fit in instead of standing out for God? What distractions or habits need to be cleared from my life in this season?

## Reflection Prayer:

God, I thank You for being the God of new beginnings. I surrender my thoughts, my plans, and my heart to You. Refresh me, realign me, and reboot my spirit so I can walk in the fullness of who You created me to be. Clear out anything in me that competes with Your voice or blocks Your direction. Today, I press reset. Not my will, but Yours be done. In Jesus' name, amen.

# Pause. Breathe.
# Write what is on your heart.

# Remember Who Holds Your Future

I can remember being about seven, playing with my neighborhood friends and talking about what we wanted to be when we grew up. I remember always wanting to be a nurse—every birthday or Christmas gift had to be a nursing instrument I could use to nurse my Cabbage Patch Kid back to life. I was adamant about caring for the sick.

Fast forward, and I'm reminded of the many church services I attended as a child when I sang the song, "He's Got the Whole World in His Hand"—not fully understanding the lyrics until I was mature enough to know who "He" was and understand the love He possessed for me. I then understood that He holds my future—and that of the world—in His hands.

Stop for a minute and think about your past, present, and future. Now ask yourself if you're holding it—or you're trusting God with it.

When we remember God's faithfulness, we find the strength to remove and reboot. He is the One who has been with us through every trial and every triumph. When we focus on His love, we're empowered to release what hinders us and step boldly into the future He has prepared.

## Scriptural Reflection:

Isaiah 43:18-19 (NIV) reminds us, "Forget the former things; do not dwell on the past. See, I am doing a new thing!"

## Spiritual Reflection:

Consider Joseph. Betrayed by his brothers, enslaved, and imprisoned, he could have been consumed by bitterness. Instead, he remembered God's faithfulness and saw his trials as preparation for something greater. In the end, God used Joseph to save nations and reconcile his family.

## Self-Reflection Question:

What promise of God do you need to remember today? What is one relationship, habit, or mindset that God may be calling you to remove, and how can you partner with Him to start the process today?

## Reflection Prayer:
Heavenly Father,

Thank You for loving me enough to want the best for me. I confess that I've held onto things You've asked me to release. Please give me the courage to remove what hinders my growth, the willingness to reboot my heart and mind, and the wisdom to remember Your love and faithfulness. Create in me a clean heart and renew a right spirit within me. Help me trust in Your plan and step boldly into the future You've prepared for me. In Jesus' name I pray. Amen.

**Pause. Breathe.
Write what is on your heart.**

# It Could Be Worse

In 2008, life felt impossible and overwhelming. I was semi-homeless, anxiously waiting to be approved for a home. My strength betrayed me as I lost the ability to lift my arms, leading to a diagnosis of myasthenia gravis, a rare autoimmune disease. To add to the weight, my mother faced an emergency double-bypass surgery, and I uprooted my life to care for her at her bedside for months—all while juggling my own health, her recovery, and the daunting process of buying a home.

In the chaos, I found myself asking, "How much worse can it get?" I knew God, prayed faithfully, leaned on my Christian support system, and trusted His Word. Yet in those moments, the truth was undeniable—I was tired, weak, and overwhelmed. I couldn't lift my arms to comb my hair or reach for anything above me. Housing bids fell through, and my resources dwindled.

But God? He didn't just hear my faint cries—He responded. Suddenly, He stepped in, not with a "by and by" answer, but with a present, tangible rescue. Today, as I look back, I can confidently say, "It could have been worse, and it could be worse." Though I still can't lift my arms to comb my hair or grab an item off the top shelf, I'm here—with arms that work in other ways. My mom is healed, I'm settled in my second home, and all is well. Only God.

## Scriptural Reflection:

Proverbs 24:16 (NIV): "For though the righteous fall seven times, they rise again, but the wicked stumble when calamity strikes."

## Spiritual Reflection:

This journey reminds me of the Apostle Paul, who pleaded with God to remove his "thorn in the flesh." Yet God's response was, "My grace is sufficient for you, for My power is made perfect in weakness" (2 Corinthians 12:9). Paul learned to boast in his weaknesses because they revealed God's strength.

## Self-Reflection Question:

When faced with overwhelming circumstances, what strengths or blessings might you be overlooking in your life? How could embracing God's sufficiency transform your perspective?

## Reflection Prayer:

Lord, thank You for sustaining me when life felt unbearable. Help me to trust in Your strength when I am weak and to see Your goodness even in my challenges. May I never forget that Your grace is sufficient for today and all my tomorrows. Amen.

# Pause. Breathe.
## Write what is on your heart.

# Don't Waste Your Grace!

Yesterday, during a conversation with my mom, I unexpectedly said, "Don't waste your grace." Those four words struck me deeply. How often do we waste what has been so freely and lovingly given?

As a society, we are very wasteful. We waste money chasing temporary happiness or social approval. We waste time on meaningless activities and relationships that add no value to our lives. We waste food, energy, and even the gifts and opportunities entrusted to us. Sadly, in doing so, we often waste the precious grace of God—a grace meant to transform, guide, and sustain us.

God's grace is not something to be taken for granted or used casually. The Apostle Paul reminds us in 2 Corinthians 6:1 not to receive God's grace in vain. When we ignore the purpose of His grace, we strip it of its intended impact on our lives. As Titus 2:11-12 teaches, God's grace is a teacher—it trains us to say no to ungodliness and to live lives marked by holiness and purpose.

Don't waste your grace—embrace it, steward it, and let it lead you to holiness!

## Scriptural Reflection:

1 Corinthians 15:10 (NIV): "But by the grace of God I am what I am, and His grace toward me was not in vain. On the contrary, I worked harder than any of them, yet not I, but the grace of God that was with me."

## Spiritual Reflection:

Consider the story of Jonah. God gave Jonah a mission, yet he wasted the initial opportunity by running away. He not only wasted time and energy, but his rebellion also endangered others. But God, in His infinite grace, gave Jonah another chance to fulfill his purpose. Jonah's story reminds us that while God's grace is abundant, it's not to be squandered. It comes with a call to action—a mission to glorify Him and grow in holiness.

## Self-Reflection Questions:

Are there areas in your life where you've been wasting God's grace? How can you intentionally use His grace to live in alignment with His purpose?

What would it look like to steward God's grace with gratitude and purpose today?

### Reflection Prayer:

Heavenly Father, thank You for the gift of Your grace. Help me to honor it by living with intention, obedience, and purpose. Teach me to steward Your grace wisely, allowing it to transform my life for Your glory. Let me never take it for granted. In Jesus' name, amen.

# Pause. Breathe.
# Write what is on your heart.

# It's Simple — WAS

The start of 2020 WAS extremely trying for me. I WAS a complete mess, feeling as if I WAS about to lose my mind. I WAS caught in the eye of a relentless storm—my marriage WAS in shambles, family feuds WERE erupting, my job WAS threatening layoffs, my refinancing paperwork WAS draining my spirit, those who once WERE my friends became foes, and my bank account WAS often sitting at or below $5.68.

BUT God! God never left me or forsook me. Even when I couldn't see or feel it, He WAS there all along, steady and faithful in the chaos.

In that storm, I WAS depleted of energy, at a loss for words daily, and barely eating, yet somehow my faith remained intact, and I slept peacefully. I held on to the belief that if I could endure and trust, everything WAS going to get better. And guess what? It did!

From that experience, I learned a profound lesson. My "WAS" was not the end—it stood for Wait-Ask-Surrender.

Let this be a reminder that no matter how challenging your "WAS" may be, it's not the end. It's an opportunity to grow, trust, and see the miraculous hand of God at work in your life.

## Scriptural Reflection:

Psalm 27:14 (NKJV): "Wait on the Lord; Be of good courage, And He shall strengthen your heart; Wait, I say, on the Lord!"

## Spiritual Reflection:

Consider Joseph, the favored son of Jacob, whose life WAS turned upside down. He WAS sold into slavery by his own brothers, falsely accused, and thrown into prison. His dreams and visions of greatness seemed shattered. Yet, in the midst of his "WAS," Joseph WAITED on God's timing, ASKED for wisdom to interpret dreams, and SURRENDERED his circumstances to the Lord. Eventually, God elevated him to second-in-command over Egypt, fulfilling the very promises He made long ago (Genesis 37-50).

Joseph's story reminds us that our "WAS" moments are never wasted. They are the soil in which God plants seeds of purpose, growth, and transformation.

## Self-Reflection Question:

Where in your life do you need to wait, ask, or surrender? Reflect on what waiting on God might look like practically in your current season. How can you shift from striving to trusting Him fully?

## Reflection Prayer:

Heavenly Father, in moments when life feels overwhelming, teach me to WAIT on You with patience and faith. Help me to ASK for Your wisdom and direction and give me the courage to SURRENDER everything I cannot control. Strengthen my heart, Lord, and remind me that Your timing is perfect. I trust You to work all things together for my good. In Jesus' name, amen.

**Pause. Breathe.
Write what is on your heart.**

# Changing Bad Behaviors

Life often leads us into habits and behaviors that may feel good at the moment but can harm us over time. These behaviors might stem from childhood influences, friendships, or societal norms. Because we live so closely with them, their harm often goes unnoticed.

And let's be honest—sometimes these behaviors do feel good. They bring temporary relief or satisfaction, masking the deeper consequences lurking beneath the surface. In the moment, the entanglement feels rewarding. It deceives us into believing we're pursuing happiness, even though we're chasing it through unhealthy means.

The truth is that what feels comfortable or "normal" is not always good for us. Sometimes, we cling to these behaviors because we don't fully know who we are. In other cases, society's definitions of "normal" lead us astray.

What we often fail to see is the hidden cost of bad behaviors. These habits can damage relationships, erode friendships, weaken self-confidence, and hinder spiritual growth. Breaking free from them requires courage and a willingness to face uncomfortable truths. True change demands identifying the behavior, understanding its root, and actively replacing it with something good.

Let this be the day you choose to step out of entanglement and into the freedom God has for you.

## Scriptural Reflection:

Ephesians 4:22-24 (CSB): "[T]o take off your former way of life, the old self that is corrupted by deceitful desires, to be renewed in the spirit of your minds, and to put on the new self, the one created according to God's likeness in righteousness and purity of the truth."

## Spiritual Reflection:

Zacchaeus (Luke 19:1-10) is a powerful example of someone who overcame bad behavior. As a tax collector, he was known for his greed and for exploiting others for personal gain. But when he encountered Jesus, everything changed. Zacchaeus acknowledged his wrongdoings, repented, and replaced his greed with generosity, boldly declaring, "If I have cheated anybody out of anything, I will pay back four times the amount." Zacchaeus's transformation shows us that no matter how deeply rooted our bad behaviors are, change is possible when we surrender to God.

## Self-Reflection Question:

What false sense of comfort or identity have you been holding on to that prevents you from becoming the person God created you to be? Are you willing to release what feels good temporarily for what is good eternally?

## Reflection Prayer:

Heavenly Father,

Thank You for Your grace and the opportunity to grow. Help me identify the habits and behaviors that are not pleasing to You. Grant me the courage to face the discomfort of change and the wisdom to replace bad behaviors with ones that honor You. I surrender my struggles to You, trusting that Your strength will guide me to transformation. In Jesus' name, amen.

**Pause. Breathe.
Write what is on your heart.**

# Embrace — You Changed

I know for certain I'd be one of the richest women in America if I got a dollar every time I heard the phrase, "**You've changed**."

One moment stands out in my memory. It was sometime in 2022 when a friend told me, through tears, that I had changed—and that my change was grieving her. She wasn't just hurt—she was mourning. Mourning the fact that I dared to grow. That I dared to obey God. That I dared to walk into a new version of myself. She literally tried to transfer her grief onto me, all because I made decisions that provoked transformation in my life.

I remember the swirl of emotions—confusion, disbelief, sadness. How could my obedience to God, my pursuit of wholeness, be so deeply misunderstood?

If you know me, you know I constantly seek God's wisdom to ensure I do no harm to His people. One of my daily prayers is, "Lord, teach me to do no harm." So hearing that my change had harmed someone shook me, and my mind went into overdrive. How can breaking bad habits, unlearning dysfunction, shifting my environment, realigning my lifestyle, and walking confidently in the gifts God entrusted to me be perceived as negative?

Let's unpack the phrase "You've changed." What does it really mean? Why is it that when people see transformation, they respond with discomfort? Could it be that our evolution exposes their stagnation? Or that our light reveals areas where they've settled in darkness?

Change, especially when driven by God, should not be feared—it should be celebrated. The Word reminds us, "And we all, who with unveiled faces contemplate the Lord's glory, are being transformed into his image with ever-increasing glory . . ." (2 Corinthians 3:18, NIV).

We were never meant to remain the same. Our walk with God demands growth. And what grieves me most is that we, as a people, often fail to celebrate that growth in others. Sometimes it seems like others would rather see you stuck in cycles of dysfunction—bound by scarcity, tied to generational strongholds—than free, whole, and rising.

But here's the truth—it costs nothing to celebrate someone else's breakthrough.

Instead of asking, "Why did you change?" perhaps the better, more loving question is, "How can I support you in your change?"

Growth is not betrayal. Elevation is not arrogance. And walking in your God-given identity is not something to apologize for. Jesus didn't suffer, bleed, and die so we could remain comfortable in mediocrity.

My prayer is that we all develop a mindset that not only welcomes transformation but also celebrates it in others. May we grow without guilt. May we change without chains. And may we walk boldly in the direction of who God is calling us to become.

## Scriptural Reflection:
Romans 12:2 (NKJV): "Do not be conformed to this world, but be transformed by the renewing of your mind, that you may prove what is that good and acceptable and perfect will of God."

## Spiritual Reflection:
Saul was known for persecuting Christians—until a divine encounter with Jesus transformed his entire identity (Acts 9). His change was so drastic that people feared it wasn't real. Yet instead of resisting, Barnabas celebrated Paul's change and helped him step into his God-ordained purpose. Paul went on to write most of the New Testament, proving that a God-ordained change will always have a Kingdom impact.

## Self-Reflection Question:
Are you resisting the change God is calling you into because of how others might perceive it?

## Reflection Prayer:
Lord, thank You for the gift of growth. Give me the courage to embrace change, even when it's misunderstood. Surround me with those who celebrate my transformation and remove anything that hinders my purpose. Let my change bring You glory. In Jesus' name, amen.

**Pause. Breathe.
Write what is on your heart.**

# It Was All a Dream

It was all a dream. I used to read *Ebony*, *Jet*, and *Essence* magazines, captivated by the famous actors and actresses gracing their covers. I would often imagine my face on one of those glossy pages. But how? Why would someone like me—a scared little girl from Louisiana—ever be featured?

Maybe the dream began to take root on a stormy night in March 2020. I was drowning in tears, caught in a violent storm—not of hail but of heartbreak and hardship. I was on the brink of divorce, facing false harassment claims, watching my finances dry up, and feeling my sense of self-worth slip away. Family drama was circling me like a pack of wolves. Amid that chaos, I clung to Psalm 27:14 (NIV): "Wait for the Lord; be strong and take heart and wait for the Lord." I repeated it over and over again—just to fall asleep, just to breathe.

Then came the whisper: *Write the book.*

I actually questioned if God had spoken to the right person. Write? Me? Lord, you know I'm my own worst critic. You know my grammar stumbles and my confidence crumbles. Still, the whisper persisted: *Write the book.*

I dismissed it and buried myself back in Psalm 27:14, trying to calm my anxious mind by convincing myself that it was just a dream—nothing more.

Weeks passed. Then a dear friend called. After our initial hello, she blurted out, "The Holy Spirit told me you have a best seller in you." I tried to explain that writing wasn't my thing, that I lacked the tools, the confidence, the clarity. She cut me off and said, "Get started, woman of God."

Then, in August 2024, my life coach (because yes—every coach needs a coach) told me on our very first call, "I see a book, and the cover is yellow." Tears ran down my face. She had no idea that yellow is my favorite color or that God had already spoken the same message. That moment confirmed what I had tried so hard to ignore.

Now, five years later, I stand at the edge of something I once thought impossible—promoting my book, *Awakened in the Mirror*.

I don't know if it will be a best seller, but I do know this—when God speaks, you must activate your faith and move, even if you feel unqualified. I've learned that God confirms His voice through others, especially when your self-doubt is loud.

So no—I'm still not fully secure in my writing. But I trust the God who called me. He edits every page of my life. He proofreads the rough drafts of my soul. He publishes purpose through my pain.

## Scriptural Reflection:

Isaiah 55:8-9 (NIV): "'For my thoughts are not your thoughts, neither are your ways my ways,' declares the Lord. 'As the Heavens are higher than the earth, so are my ways higher than your ways and my thoughts than your thoughts.'"

## Spiritual Reflection:

Remember Moses? He doubted himself too. He told God he was slow of speech and not the right man for the job (Exodus 4:10). But God reminded him, "Now go; I will help you speak and will teach you what to say" (Exodus 4:12, NIV). What a powerful reminder that our limitations never limit God.

## Self-Reflection Question:

What dream have you been sitting on because you think you're not ready, not skilled, or not enough—and what would shift if you trusted that God already equipped you before He called you?

## Reflection Prayer:

Lord, thank You for calling me even when I doubted myself. Strengthen my faith to move forward when You speak. Teach me to trust Your timing, Your voice, and Your power. Let my story bring healing and hope to others. I surrender the pen to You. In Jesus' name, amen.

# Pause. Breathe.
# Write what is on your heart.

# Scared Little Girl from Louisiana

Now, as I close these chapters, my prayer is that something inside you has been awakened—that you will not only seek God but also chase His will and embrace change. And remember this truth—if you don't move, you won't move.

I know what it feels like to hesitate. I was the girl scared to move. Afraid of failing. Nervous about what people might say. Held hostage by doubt. Waiting for the perfect timing and a flawless path. And while I waited, doors opened . . . and closed. Opportunities came . . . and went. Prayers circled the same words, but my feet stayed still.

Then the mirror called me out. I had to face the question: Do I have what it takes to do what God has placed in me? Write the book? Launch the business? Step into early retirement? Live fully in His purpose?

And in the stillness, I heard Him say: *"Move."*

That's when I learned—faith is not faith without movement. When God says move, He is not only with you in the move—He's already at the destination, preparing the way.

So today, as another year comes to a close, this scared little girl from Louisiana is no longer standing still. I moved. I chased His will. And I can tell you this—obedience unlocked more than I ever dreamed. It's been ABSOLUTELY AMAZING.

## Scriptural Reflection:

2 Timothy 1:7 (KJV): "For God has not given us a spirit of fear, but of power and of love and of a sound mind."

## Spiritual Reflection:

Like Moses, fear made me want to shrink back. Moses argued with God: "Who am I? What if they don't listen? I can't speak well" (Exodus 3–4). But when he moved—despite his fear—he walked into miracles. Fear didn't stop God's plan—obedience set it in motion.

## Reflective Prayer:

Lord, replace my fear with faith. Help me move boldly into what You've called me to, knowing You have already gone before me. Amen.

## Life-Coach Charge:

Stop waiting for perfect conditions. Stop rehearsing the "what-ifs." The time is now. The question is—what bold move will you commit to making today that aligns you with God's will and activates your next chapter?

*Your Affirmation:*
I will no longer stand still in fear—God has called me to move, and I move with faith, courage, and purpose.

www.ingramcontent.com/pod-product-compliance
Lightning Source LLC
Chambersburg PA
CBHW070454100426
42743CB00010B/1621